Grass W
&
The Plague Stone

Grass Widow
&
The Plague Stone

JONATHAN WAIN

THE PENTLAND PRESS LTD
Edinburgh Cambridge Durham USA

© Jonathan Wain, 1999

First published in 1999 by
The Pentland Press Ltd
Hutton Close
South Church
Bishop Auckland
Durham

All rights reserved.
Unauthorised duplication
contravenes existing laws.

ISBN : 1 85821 626 5

Typeset and printed
by Lintons Printers, County Durham

I would like to dedicate this book to Sophie

Grass Widow

Jonathan Wain

THE GRASS WIDOW

What an estranged life we must lead
Looking at it from the outside
Some days I'm avoiding you
Others it couldn't be further from the truth
Some days I've left her indoors behind
Seeking any solace I can find
Some nights it's been sheer delight
No end of rows but little fight
Some fuck-ups for sure
Honestly there could have been more
I do try to love you
What are we going to do?
Nothing probably will have to do
As we go up and down the motorway a thousand times
Other people don't need our strife
You are always around when I get back from my travels
Maybe a string of pearls for a heart attack
We run quite well on the whole
A string of pearls for a special girl

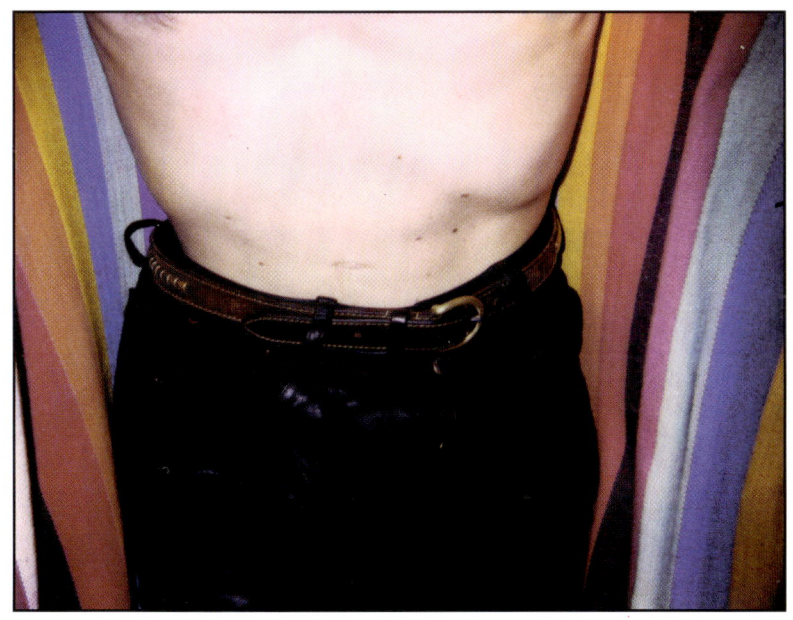

MIRAGE

It's a mirage you'll never make it
Unless you head for your goals
Endless endless bloody pitfalls
We'll finish with it and go abroad
Some people are no help at all
Over two thousand years old and
                        trading jewels
Universal language for a ship of fools
A room full of icons
For those who believe
Torah tarot does not deceive me
The good come back again I suppose
To lord it over the Earth who knows
Perhaps not invisible I would say
Unfortunately some want to keep
                        it that way
The dawn of time should move
                        you away

Egypt or Genesis is fine in the end
Taken some prisoners
Fond of the Mary Chain
A woman forgiven
And one not again
A year with a lioness
Like a wyvern I fly
Who's granted my rings I can't
                        decide
Good enough for your finger to be
                        chopped off it's true
You'd stay out of trouble if I were
                        you
Over two thousand years old and
                        trading jewels
Universal language for a ship of fools

THE GRANDE GRIMORE

A dictionary I have found on my travels its true
Mostly time in prayer the rest of the deck
How I came by my cards I will never forget
Work found in Knightsbridge
Via the Empress success
Power starts in Goa and ends up in the West
In a carpet shop in Piccadilly
Love from the Mystery Round but indolence too
Abundance and luxury far later it's true
My two aces from villages to the north
A goddess presiding for what it's worth
The elements mastered on one sunny day
A whirlwind approaches to sweep you away
Leaving not a desert in its wake
But a treasure house of images
A magician by that stage
A house that moves - Beth
I've got all the good bits the rest is like death

'Work found in Knightsbridge'

'Via the Express success'

'Power starts in Goa and ends up in the West'

Abundance chewed slightly

'My two aces from villages to the North
A goddess presiding for what it's worth'

'The elements mastered on one sunny day'

'A magician by that stage'

LIFE
All perfectly legal my spells
Power in the kitchen
And in the Dining Room Wealth
Better stay on Gain though
Ask the Master he should know
By my bed some big black books
I wrote one myself
See the trouble I took
A wicked witch flies through the skies
Very buckled at the knees
Enough Magick to knock your socks off
Still never good enough
I give up
On my last adventure I brought some treasure back
Life in socks I can relax

LONDON

Two sisters and a heart attack
Not impossible to get back
A floor upon which to crash
Breaking the hearts of young virgins
I revolve around that record again
Unwanted strong girl and I
A box of chocolates I'll remember hopefully
Some very different approaches to reality
In the capable hands of five supermodels
Our divorce isn't final yet apparently no decent men
Start scouring Europe as part of the battle plan
Perhaps there are problems I can hold it up
Drift off into Magick though quite good at cups
Cache of swords we found by comparison can't be helped
                                                            tough!

'Cache of swords we found by comparison can't be helped tough!'

SATAN

High speed gallop through the year as usual
The map looks fine at least vaguely interesting
You late back on the boat black tie in full swing
Beyond you in the distance we the Naphilim
Picnic on the lawn for us in the end
Sold views by Satan things can get quite threatening
Kingdoms and Dominions rescued by angels
Urns made of marble skies dark and forboding
Not sure what you are capable of by comparison
Escape clause I bought a dictionary of fun bits
The past well documented the future awaiting
Some things unwanted but that is what happened
Some things quite popular LION even for vegetarians
Reworking my scribble every single lunchtime
Can't photograph half the things I'm interested in
Back to the Drawing Board again

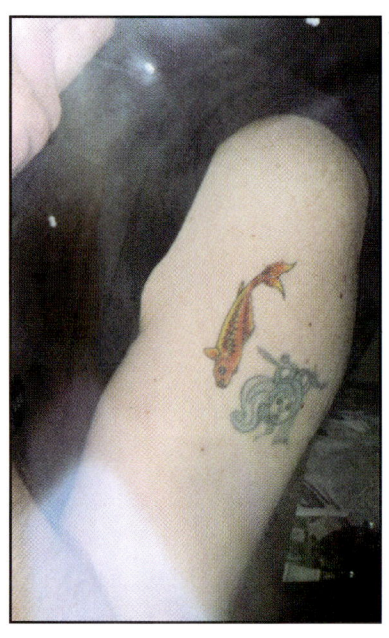

MY ORDER
Even alone I prop up the bar
Quite used to the name Scar
Most have seen the Lion King
Goldfish by lunch
I get her all day
Allowed to check on supper
We get on okay
More people by night
I have to send them away
Destined to travel the State
Swordplay I fight my corner
Band of gypsies
Storyteller
Not running out
I fashioned a spell
Perhaps we can do going quite well
Abroad we can forget it
A horse at weekends

LIFE TOO

Train fares a taxi a car in the end
I move from bed to bed it never ends
A squeeze on the bum perhaps
Cover the miles
Organised I can decide
The end of my life is sorted
Perhaps fired a few more times
Swordplay perhaps I hit the church at Easter
I don't blame you Christ
Grateful enough
Enemies in the wake of a million falls
I know I know I've hit brick walls
Clean and tidy I tart things up
She prefers it to be honest

HELLO! SPECIAL

Finding words to picture
I ravage my chest
What is today like I'll have to guess
Cards flying away in the breeze
Tall statues quite different at best
Polish my sword I enjoy acting Hell's Angel
Housing estate rules wicked witch not appreciated
Mass murderer obviously animal husbandry
Highly impressive not enough marketing
Very repetitive drifting off constantly
Finishing my deck a good Hello! piece probably
Refuse to surrender vegetables eventually
Choose blissful ignorance blessed with insanity
A phonebook full of accidents all summer I've vanished
Not completely impossible somehow we've managed
Refuse to lie down big time nobody

SIGNAL MY BURIAL
A wish granted perhaps
Slighly removed and finally happy
A black widow spider moves mountains
Trying to get to me
Two families at war in love and hate it seems
No sooner daffodils and I'm out to grass
Trying to avoid a kick up the ass
Very tall statues watch it pass
A thousand falls more floors at last
Scratch your bloody eyes out please bow out with grace
Wouldn't want to wreck that pretty face
The underworld possibly certainly not the rat race
Truce after some work a document to present
Love and kisses at last some fun in the end

'No sooner daffodils and I'm out to grass'

HAPPY
Poetry constitutes work I'm allowed to sit and rhyme
Vast house with pillars by the oracle I swore
Can you predict us I can't anymore

HAPPY

In another tower at bed
She's in another wing my friend
Seriously boring I snore in the end
I can tell she's beside me most of the time
Poetry constitutes work I'm allowed to sit and rhyme
Vast house with pillars by the oracle I swore
Can you predict us I can't anymore
It's interesting though
Quite beautiful really as someone else said
I travel at will now is it worth seventy-five miles again?
Of course it is I enjoy it in the end
We both need a lot of space you and I
Grant you half LONDON over which to preside
From a fairytale castle that has to budget at times
Prince Charming rides

DIMINISHING RESPONSIBILITY

Perhaps it was Genesis in the end
Great bands in Nod meet up with some friends
Maybe she's quite happy in the World of Men
I escaped via the Nephilim there is magick amen
'As you like it' slightly our story at the moment
Flat broke with Celia Forest of Arden no longer a baddie
Deaf in one ear we can figure out the lovers probably
Hold on to your horses Imperial Marriage
Junk shop the salesman from Mr Ben plenty of treasure
Harmless and innocent find someone else then

STEALTH

Fly by stealth at night I do
Perhaps a witch on a broomstick
Back and forth as I wish
London or the countryside again
Ferrying jewels
Treasures more what great delight
Got the city in my sight
Some trade tonight
Drag back my hoard
Liable to get bored
So more work perhaps
Perhaps I go again quite soon
Escape remains here for a Loony Tune
Fly around at will in the end
Punch on the nose mercenary I get about
Carpet sales I'll take you out
The lap of luxury rings more bells for me
Than ending up in misery

THRESHOLD
Amazed I don't have to wield my sword too much
Just a punch in the throat is usually enough
Plans carried out with little fuss
Tombraider in Imajica I roam
Time to rest though
Perhaps I've got enough stuff
Time to manipulate it
Stumble through the Book of Days
As always
Is it a diary of the year?
Or how I found it is not clear

TRIGGER

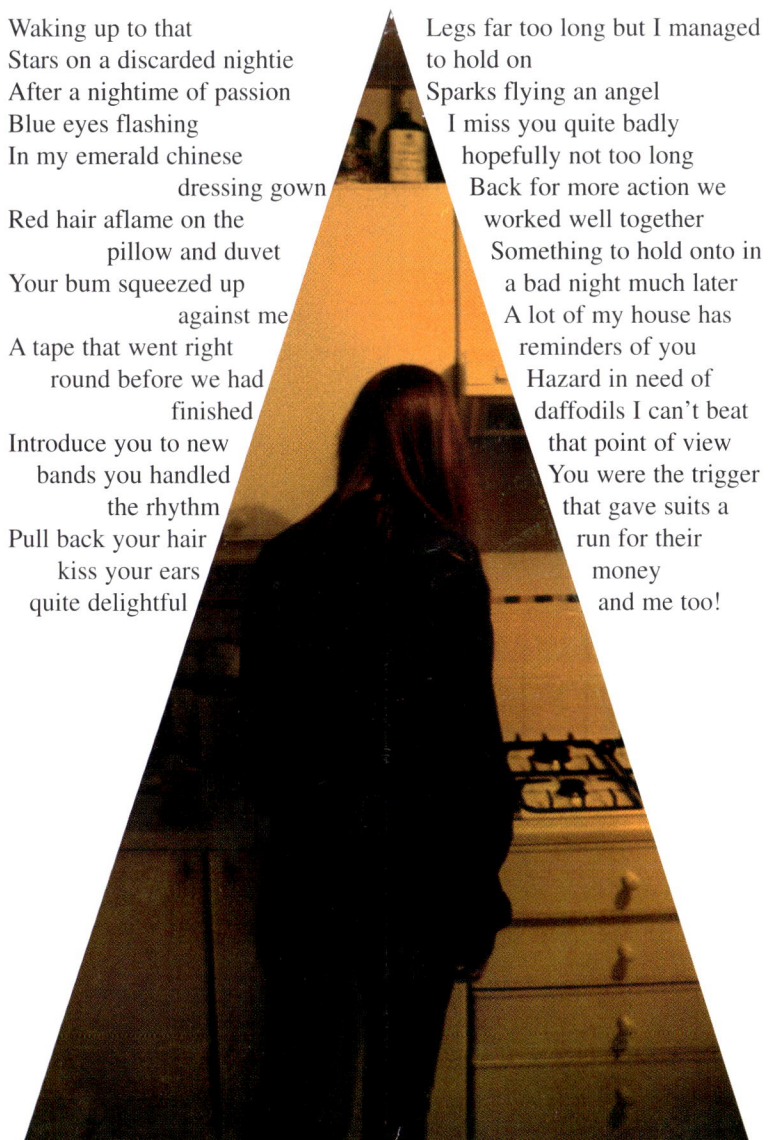

Waking up to that
Stars on a discarded nightie
After a nightime of passion
Blue eyes flashing
In my emerald chinese
   dressing gown
Red hair aflame on the
   pillow and duvet
Your bum squeezed up
   against me
A tape that went right
   round before we had
   finished
Introduce you to new
   bands you handled
   the rhythm
Pull back your hair
   kiss your ears
   quite delightful

Legs far too long but I managed
   to hold on
Sparks flying an angel
I miss you quite badly
   hopefully not too long
Back for more action we
   worked well together
Something to hold onto in
   a bad night much later
A lot of my house has
   reminders of you
Hazard in need of
   daffodils I can't beat
   that point of view
You were the trigger
   that gave suits a
   run for their
   money
   and me too!

The Duke of Beaufort's Panther and Wyvern

WYVERN

As the Panther and the Wyvern in the end
Not compatible at all perhaps it's a godsend
Some good bits perhaps but on the whole not nice
The Wyvern vanishes in a trice
The Panther insists on going downhill
I can't support that I never will
It's over now we've all given up hope
Bringing you up to scratch is a joke
I don't need the war I've got weapons enough
You'll never figure me out your life will be tough
By comparison I'm an incentive scheme
After all we are allowed to dream
Fertility rings bells in the end I'm afraid

CADUCEUS

There's lunch in my company
You can ring round for the nights
Cheetah or leopard usually zebra sometimes
My executive director thinks I should retire
I only get the moon once a month these days
I shouldn't listen to her
Her indoors too slightly but we've managed a year
I'm happy at last
Quite how isn't clear
Might have to give up the car and go in by bus
Maybe it is not worth all the fuss
People keep trying to spoil all the things I enjoy
Perhaps I surrender I've got medals for bravery

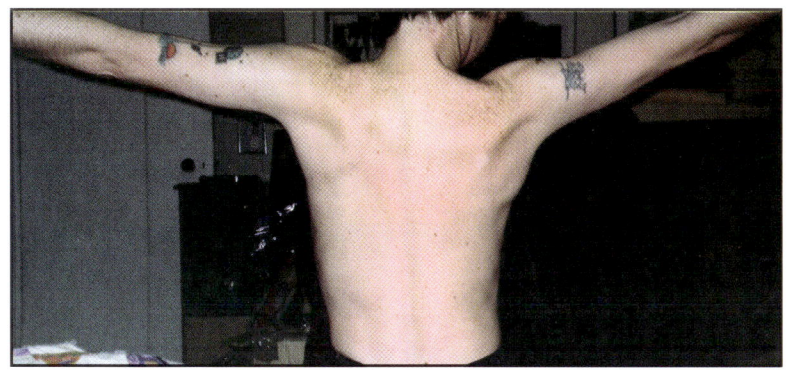

PROPPING THE HOUSE UP
Fired to be installed in a management position
One hoop per day I'm a hopeless afternoon
Frequently swords living with a battleaxe
Finally strong enough to survive on my own
In the end communion possibly hundreds of people
Out of bed the right side not remotely ropey
Tug of war for strength obviously
Charlie finds his way to our front room
Curiously enough a passport to everybody
Messenger by comparison endless little wars
Life on coke if absolutely necessary
Left in the capable hands of women my board
Dragged down to your level bird of prey vanishing eagle
Not exactly brilliant but better than nothing
Around the goldfish wakes up every few seconds
Newts in the pond a garden exploding in colour
Knight of Wands eventually fire sign Salamander

TWO HOUSES

Over here in Nephythys we don't do very much
They're always running out in Isis
Behind bars we're stuck
There is time off though
Slightly wondering why there is so much fuss
Running around in circles anyway fucks me up
Usually the bars are the kind I prop up
Quite ragged though I generally slope off
A punch on the nose shuts most people up
Into a baddie I turn they want me dead
Perhaps not commercial at all in the end
This is how it runs though
I still meet the other side but we avoid mortal blows

ART

Spiked between One and Three
In a taxi of light
We can finally afford it can we
Enough time in the day for work at last
You bring me my breakfast
Black coffee with a little cold water
Is all the doctor will allow
Power
Love
Optimism
I'm a carpet salesman now
A tower house with stained glass
Paying the bills kicks me up the arse
That woman grabs me by the balls
Drags me round the shops and food halls
I enjoy it though

SALESMAN

One woman at lunch
And four for the night
Maintenance going out of sight
A chairman drifting into cups
A board of directors that never give up
Some interesting fairytales
Some spectacular deaths
a routine that has settled down
Life out amongst the Nephilim
Six hundred products that never sell
One does quite well
Still stuck in my book a muse perhaps Deathstrike
A night out is suddenly seventy-five miles away
Come and stay!

MAGAZINE

Magazine I adore you
With my snake hips
Here to score you

Magazine how you thrill me
In your heels
Just dressed to kill me

Magazine how you thrill me
In your leathers
To outskill me!

Come wander in my garden
And feel thoughts start to harden
From a dream

Magazine!

Magazine how you chill me
With your adverts
Out to kill me
Magazine!

The Plague Stone

Jonathan Wain

THE PLAGUE STONE
As the seasons of the year unfold
A horse put out to grass
Watch the daffodils ripen and grow old
Get the vegetables up and start my horse again
He'll be spooking at trees at first
I've been to endless planets
I collapse amongst my cushions
Smoke clouds Venus quite serene
A voyage round the moon I've seen
A garden party and a Hunt Ball
A day at the Races I see it all
The Plague Stone marks my territory
Against it I often wee
Jupiter and Mercury
I've hunted Neptune and Mars of course
Most end under Saturn but I went further north
Pluto perhaps the Sun in the end
Uranus is a bad mistake
I leave some money that the lepers take

TREASURE
Two pewter goblets and some prison bars
A dinner party : life on Mars
A tiara for a princess
Days like this obviously blessed
Lichen and moss on stone balls
She arrives at last I've been set free
Plenty of scent with the ghost and me
Totter around in your heels
We manage it relatively easily
Cabbage with our evening meal
Carrots soon and Iceberg too spinach and potato
                                          plenty of good food

MY HAND

Moved from a queen of spades to a queen of hearts
I can inflict some damage if we're playing Hearts
On bridge though there is simply no bid
All the court cards have been hid
A void in spades besides the ten
Mind you I've found strength again
The queen of spades against me then
A rifle round the upper deck
The nine of clubs I won't forget
A lot to lose
The ten of diamonds I suppose
The court of the King and Queen of Swords as Dylan said
A fire sign instead
A landlord in the end
Curious how life maps out
You'll grow up with speed under your belt my friend
A generous uncle to drive you round the bend

'A void in spades besides the ten'

'Mind you I found strength again'

'The Queen of Spades against me then'

'You'll grow up with speed under your belt my friend'

'A generous uncle to drive you round the bend'

VISHNU AT THE AXLETREE

After much persuasion
Night after three
I let Hanuman take me to the Axletree
And with its boughs reaching
To all sides of the quadrangle
There indeed many stars did see
Zodiac Galaxy
Linked from every angle
Seated on the spiky grass carpetry
With our backs to its trunk

Returning home to sleep with Eve
Immersed in cosmic fantasy
Her body lithe in ecstasy
Awaiting
And The monster there was me, too

LOVE

The carpet is called love
Blim burns on a Kashmiri rug
Set on fire
Its crewel stitch
Reminds me of you you bitch
Memories of chilling out
Even now it transforms my house
Isis my love

CHESS

Right across the board a pair of bishops
Solid fortune without hiccups
We talk at tangents on the whole
Moving on diagonals
Serving up a harmless day
Animals at bay
The wheels of fortune had stood still
When we change horses until
We narrow down upon your King
The panther forces surrender of your Queen
Castles of air float into night
We'll find you somewhere without much ado
Happily wandering the lower deck
A ring of fire my desire
A challenge for you
A weeks notice before I move my King

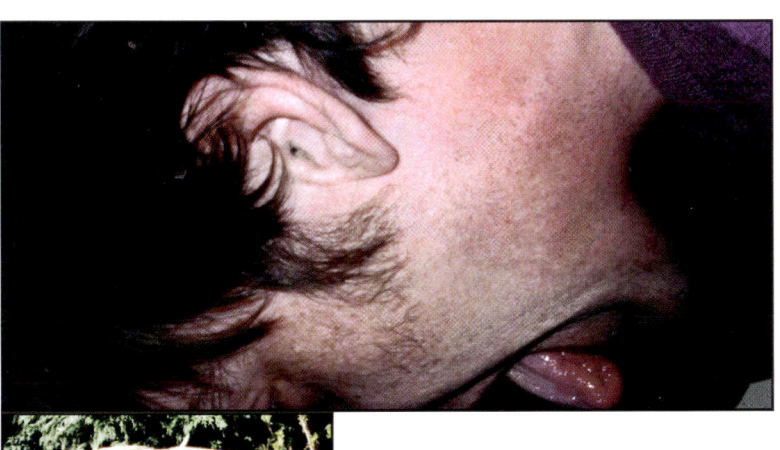

ROUTINE

Away on business all the time it seems
Stuck in the office trading dreams
Furious negotiations
Station to station
It's her that answers back not she
The limitless light getting used to me
Seeking completion for this deal
Perhaps less gloss paint
Perhaps more real
Light relief my friend
A sister of mercy on whom to depend
Her a grieving for me
She a maze can do it easily
Across the board she sweeps
The jester sleeps but the raven peeps

FULL CRY
As dawn rises
Looking through the ears of a horse
The finest view in England of course
She's reading a book in due course
The pub for lunch as well
Back for last orders to a round of applause
We can just make it if we hurry
Cut glass crystal an order tall
Agatha Christie in the conservatory
Arsenic in my coffee
There are pop songs at the ball
Not really stuffy at all
Gored to death by hounds a boar
Above my bed next to the sword